Cor

D0887268

Heather Hammonds

Corn

Do you like to eat corn?
Corn grows on tall corn plants.
Corn plants are grown in many places
around the world.

Corn is found in many different foods we eat.
Corn is made into animal food, too.

Corn is also made into other things.

silk

cob

kernels

fuel

husk

3

Corn Story

Corn plants are a kind of grass.
They grow in summer
when the weather is warm and sunny.

People have been growing corn plants
for thousands of years.

Corn was first grown in Mexico. People ate fresh corn and made flour from corn seeds.

Soon people from other countries began to grow corn, too.

Corn is also called maize.

Chapter 3

Kinds of Corn

There are many different kinds of corn plants.

Some plants grow corn
that makes good flour.

Some plants grow sweet corn
that is good to eat.

corn flour

Some plants grow corn that is made into food for people and animals.

Some plants grow corn that makes good popcorn!

chicken feed

popcorn

Corn can be yellow.
It can be other colors, too.

Chapter 4

Corn Farms

Most corn is grown on farms.

Some corn is grown on small farms.
Farmers:

till the soil

plant the corn seeds

harvest the corn

Some corn is grown on huge farms.

Farmers use big machines to:
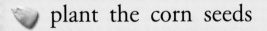 till the soil

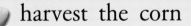 plant the corn seeds   harvest the corn

Chapter 5

Planting the Seeds

It is spring at this big corn farm.
It is time to plant the corn seeds.

The corn fields are tilled.

They are watered with big **sprinklers**.

tilling the corn fields

The corn seeds are planted in long rows.
Plant food is put into the soil at the same time.

Sometimes weed and insect killers
are put into the soil, too.

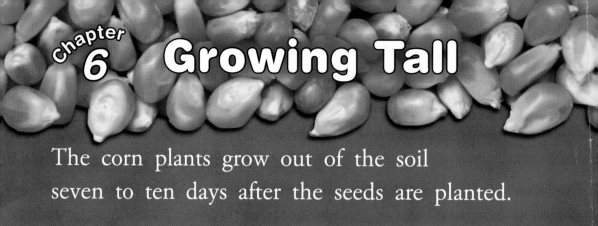

Chapter 6

Growing Tall

The corn plants grow out of the soil seven to ten days after the seeds are planted.

The plants are watered again as they grow. They are given more plant food, too.

When the weather is warm,
the corn plants grow fast.
The rows of corn are weeded with a machine.

Soon the corn plants
are taller than the farmer!

A corn plant needs:
- warm weather
- water
- fertilizer
- good soil
- weed killer
- **insecticide**

Chapter 7

Tassels and Silks

It is summer on the farm.

Tassels grow on top of the corn plants.

Little **ears** of corn
grow on the stalks.
Lots of thin **silks**
grow from the ears of corn.

silks

Pollen from the tassels
falls down onto the silks.
Then the corn begins to
grow inside the ears.

You can see
lots of corn silks
inside this **corncob**.

Chapter 8

Harvesting the Corn

The corn grows bigger and bigger.
Soon there are lots of little kernels on each cob.
It is time to harvest the corn.

It takes around 70 to 100 days
before corn is ready to harvest.

Big machines cut the corn plants
and take the ears of corn from the stalks.
The corn plants are left behind in the corn field.

Some harvesting machines
can also take the kernels
off the corncobs.

17

9 After Harvest

The corn from this farm is sweet corn.
After harvesting, it is sent to market.

Sweet corn can also be canned or frozen at factories.

Other kinds of corn are sent to factories and made into other things.

At some farms, cornstalks are harvested, too.

The cornstalks are used for animal food.

After the corn harvest is over,
the farmer may let his cows eat the old cornstalks.
Then the fields are plowed again.

a field of old cornstalks

The farmer grows hay in the cornfields
in autumn and winter.
More corn will be planted next spring!

Chapter 11

Grow Your Own Corn

You can grow your own corn.
You will need:

- warm weather
- a place to grow the corn
- plant food
- water
- corn seeds

Plant your corn seeds in rows,
just like farmers do.
Give them lots of water and plant food.
When the corn is ready, you can eat it!

Glossary

corncob — the hard stalk inside an ear of corn, on which kernels grow

ears — parts of corn plants that contain the corn silks, corncobs, and kernels

harvest — to pick a crop of plants when they are ripe

insecticide — chemicals used to kill insects

pollen — tiny grains from a plant that make plant fruit grow

silks — long thin threads that grow inside an ear of corn

sprinklers — machines that spread water over plants

tassels — parts of a corn plant that grow at the top of the plant, have many tiny flowers, and spread pollen

till — to dig in or plow the soil

Index